WORDS

**They Got You Into This—
They Can Get You Out!**

Steve Caronna

WORDS: They Got You Into This—They Can Get You Out!
Copyright 2022 by Steve Caronna

Critical Mass Books
Haymarket, Virginia
www.criticalmasspublishing.com

1st Edition
ISBN: 978-1-947153-38-7

Cover Design   Eowyn Riggins
Interior Layout   Rachel Newhouse

Acknowledgements

I must begin by thanking my wonderful wife, Connie. Not only did she read through this manuscript and give me valuable advice, but God knew I needed a life mate and soul mate who would keep my head and heart straight. Thank you, Connie—I love you.

Thank you also to David R. Stokes and Critical Mass Publishing for their patience and guidance throughout the journey on this project. Publishing a book is no easy task, they made the process uncomplicated and rewarding.

Thank you to the ever-encouraging Heather Lee for reviewing this manuscript and for her valuable and "uncomfortably" candid advice.

It's so important to me to have people in my life who are called to lead and develop others. I'm thankful for our pastors,

Micah and Melissa Caronna who pray for Connie and me, challenge us, and are Godly examples of what it means to value others and make sacrifices so that others may know the Truth.

Most importantly, I would like to thank the Holy Spirit who guided me to and through this project—sometimes whispering, *"This is the way, walk in it"* (Is. 30:21). There just aren't words to express how much I value His Guidance in in my life! —SC

About the Author

With over 40 years of pastoral and ministry experience, Steve Caronna is actively involved in helping people discover the power of God's Word. Through books, church services, and conferences, Steve wants to encourage us to be overcomers in every situation.

Steve has his Bachelor of Arts degree in theology, and a Master's degree in pastoral studies. When he and his wife Connie aren't traveling for ministry, he enjoys golfing and fly fishing.

Contact Steve Caronna at: Stevec@lwfc.org

Introduction

Bill Smith has recently had his share of challenges. He was let go from his job two years ago after working for his company for twelve years. Not only was he without a job for 14 months, but he and his wife both ended up in the hospital with COVID 19—although at different times. They faced financial challenges during that time, especially with their son still in college.

The good news is that both of them have fully recovered, and late last year Bill landed an even better position than he had before. His new co-workers really enjoy being around him because of his *positive attitude*. His wife will tell you that Bill has always been positive, even in the toughest of circumstances. Their son has now graduated from college, his education paid for mostly by his parents, and is living on his own. Life is getting back to "normal", and they're leaving soon on their first vacation in two years.

Adam Johnson has almost had the identical set of circumstances. Two years ago he also was dismissed from the company he had worked at for eleven years, but he is still without a job. It wasn't difficult for his boss to decide who to cut from the staff, because of Adam's chronic *negativity*. His attitude was even mentioned when his boss was contacted for a reference. His wife is supporting both of them while he continues to search for meaningful work. But so far, nothing is available that would compensate him for the engineering career for which he trained.

His wife spent two weeks in the hospital recovering from pneumonia, and even though she was discharged six months ago, she's still having breathing issues. Their son came home from college four months ago to help by getting a job at a local restaurant, because the family couldn't keep up with his education expenses.

He only had six months until graduation.

What could have made the difference in these two families?

"Death and life are in the power of the tongue, and those who love it will eat its fruit" —Prov. 18:21

Contents

ONE

"Failure-Proof Living"

"Death and life are in the power of the tongue, And those who love it will eat its fruit." —Proverbs 18:21

Words matter. In fact, they are a matter of life and death. That's what the Bible teaches us. The Message paraphrase of Proverbs 18:21 says, *"Words kill, words give life; they're either poison or fruit—you choose."*

Words can create an atmosphere in and around us. Almost everyone knows a person who brings life to those around them. They can bring encouragement into a room full of people that were discouraged. We feel hope return just by being in their presence. How do they do that?

They do it with words—what they speak.

People respond to us according to the words, phrases, and even tone that comes out of our mouths. As we will see in this book, people will be lifted up, and even our circumstances will change when we learn the power in our words. This verse in Proverbs chapter 18 even says that we need to learn to love the fruit of life that our words produce.

Most of the mistakes we make in life either begin with words or significantly involve them. Whether premeditated or spontaneously uttered, our words can quickly become toxic. And like a contagious virus, they can infect those around us— especially those we love. Most of us wouldn't think of exposing others to bacteria, the kind that could make them sick, and we do our best to avoid spreading germs. We are conscious that breath could contain infectious microbes. Similarly, when we blurt something out without thinking, it can be like a virus-dense sneeze.

But do we ever consider what we expose people to with our words?

Our words don't even have to be mean or malicious to negatively impact others. Just communicating frustration about something can create an atmosphere that drags our friends and loved ones down. When you say something negative to your spouse, guess what happens? She's soon in the pit with you.

Life is in the power of our words—and so is death. Life or death to our marriages, our careers, our finances, even our health is decided upon by the words that we speak. With so much failure around us, don't you want to bring success to your life? To your relationships? To your environment? I'm ready to stop failing and start succeeding, aren't you? Of course, you are.

Have you ever thought about how to make your life failure-proof? The Apostle Peter wrote two books in the New Testament, the second of which gives us some clues about how to failure-proof our lives. Here's how he began that epistle:

> *Grace and peace be multiplied to you in the knowledge*
> *of God and of Jesus our Lord, as His divine power has*
> *given to us all things that pertain to life and godliness,*
> *through the knowledge of Him who called us by glory*
> *and virtue, by which have been given to us exceedingly*
> *great and precious promises, that through these you may*

be partakers of the divine nature, having escaped the corruption that is in the world through lust.

But also for this very reason, giving all diligence, add to your faith virtue, to virtue knowledge, to knowledge self-control, to self-control perseverance, to perseverance godliness, to godliness brotherly kindness, and to brotherly kindness love. For if these things are yours and abound, you will be neither barren nor unfruitful in the knowledge of our Lord Jesus Christ. For he who lacks these things is shortsighted, even to blindness, and has forgotten that he was cleansed from his old sins.

Therefore, brethren, be even more diligent to make your call and election sure, for if you do these things you will never stumble; for so an entrance will be supplied to you abundantly into the everlasting kingdom of our Lord and Savior Jesus Christ. —II Peter 1:2-11 (NKJV)

Notice the phrase, *"if you do these things, you will never stumble."* The Greek work for stumble is *Ptaio*, and it means to fail or make a mistake. So, Peter is telling us that if we do certain things—these things he has itemized—we can stop making mistakes. We can stop doing dumb and destructive things.

4

Of course, it's unrealistic to expect to live perfect lives and never make a mistake. But just like the best professional golfer who never hits all of the shots in a round perfectly, they still pursue the perfect game. Think about it—every professional golfer, even one who makes millions on the PGA Tour every year, still has coaches, and is in search of an even better game with fewer mistakes. In the same way, we should take this passage to heart and allow the Bible to "coach" us in pursuit of better, powerful, fulfilling, and effective lives.

How many of us would like to stop making mistakes? We have all made more mistakes than we care to admit—mistakes with our money, health, or even in our marriages. But Peter, a man who literally walked with Jesus, encourages us that if we do "these things," we can stop failing and start succeeding.

What are "these things?" He spells them out in the preceding verses. And here is how it reads in the *Amplified Bible*:

> *"For this very reason, adding your diligence [to the divine promises], employ every effort in exercising your faith to develop virtue (excellence, resolution, Christian energy), and in [exercising] virtue [develop] knowledge (intelligence), And in [exercising] knowledge [develop] self-control, and in [exercising] self-control [develop]*

steadfastness (patience, endurance), and in [exercising] steadfastness [develop] godliness (piety), And in [exercising] godliness [develop] brotherly affection, and in [exercising] brotherly affection [develop] Christian love."

Peter makes something quite clear here—each value builds on the one before it, gradually growing to the ultimate place of brotherly affection and Christian love. So, we use faith to develop excellence, and so forth. But to build knowledge, we don't start with brotherly love. We don't start at the top and work our way down. Love is not the starting point—it's the goal.

It's the icing on the cake of our character.

We need to begin with the foundation, which means we start with faith. We then take that faith and use it to develop energetic excellence. Then we use that faith and excellence to develop knowledge and so forth, cumulatively, until we get to the top, which is operating in the Love of God.

For example, take self-control. How many of us have tried to exercise self-control without the faith or knowledge to support it? How about self-control in our eating habits? How many of us have decided in frustration that we need to lose weight, but we didn't have the faith or the spirit of excellence or the knowledge to know what we were doing, so the diet was short-lived?

Each of these steps builds on the other—like a godly snowball effect.

The reason I share this is because the power of our words has everything to do with laying that vital foundation of faith. In Hebrews 11:1, it says, *"Now faith is the substance of things hoped for the evidence of things not seen."* The Amplified Bible says faith *"perceives as [real] fact what is not yet revealed to our senses."* And in the very next verse we read, *"By it, the elders obtained a good testimony."*

Here the Bible mentions elders. It's not only organizational charts and graphs, and the ability to delegate that make a good leader. Leaders must have a strong testimony of walking by faith.

In Hebrews 11:3, the Amplified Bible says, *"By faith we understand that the worlds [during the successive ages] were framed (fashioned, put in order, and equipped for their intended purpose) by the word of God, so that what we see was not made out of things which are visible."*

It is important to remember that this whole idea of walking by faith, as well as the creative power of words, were God's idea, and He demonstrated it by creating the universe. The passage makes it clear that the world wasn't formed out of nothing, but that He "framed" it by His Word. His Word literally filled space. And it's the same with our words—they take up actual space in the universe.

Words are *things* containing creative ability.

In the very first words in the Bible, we are confronted with God's creative ability. It says, *"In the beginning, God created the heavens and the earth, and the earth was without form and void and darkness was on the face of the deep. And the spirit of God was hovering over the face of the waters."* The Spirit of God was literally suspended and incubating, brooding, and setting the tone for God to move. But notice closely—nothing happened until God *spoke*.

You see, the Holy Spirit can be on the scene in a local church every Sunday morning, but nothing happens until somebody *speaks*.

The Holy Spirit is in your home, your car, and with you, wherever you are, and wherever you go. But nothing happens until you speak His Word in faith.

8

In Genesis chapter one, verse three, God said, "*Let there be light*," and light appeared. It didn't come from nothing but rather from the power of His words. We need to move past the notion that God created the universe out of nothing. It's not true. He created it out of the power of His words.

In Genesis chapter one, verse eight, God said, *"Let there be a firmament,"* and in verse nine, He said, *"Let the waters under the heavens be gathered together."* In verse eleven, God said, *"Let the earth bring forth grass,"* and in verse fourteen, He said, *"Let there be lights in the firmament."* He spoke those things into existence with nothing more than His words.

As you read this, I want to challenge you to change your mindset. If you will decide today to grow in this, you won't just be speaking words of *hope* anymore-you'll be speaking words of *faith*. You won't have to say, "one day I hope my finances get straightened out," or "one day when this medicine cures me." Whatever your situation, your goal should be to get to the point where you're walking by faith consistently and speaking God's Word into every part of your life. Don't be concerned that you don't know how to do that yet. That's what this book is about, and I'm going to teach you how to do exactly that.

---

[1] Proverbs 18:21 (NKJV)

[2] II Peter 1:1-12 (NIV)

[3] Galatians 5:22-23 (NIV)

[4] Genesis 1:1-2 (NKJV)

TWO

"Faith Speaks"

Verse three of Hebrews chapter one is powerful: *"who being the brightness of His glory and the express image of His person, and upholding all things by the word of His power, when He had by Himself purged our sins, sat down at the right hand of the Majesty on high...".*

Did you catch that? *"Upholding all things by the word of His power."* The word "uphold" in the Greek translation implies God is *sustaining, guiding,* and *propelling* all things by the power of His Word. The Amplified Bible's take on this verse says, *"upholding, maintaining, guiding, and propelling the universe by his mighty word of power."* Jesus didn't just create the universe by His spoken word, but He continues to maintain it with that same powerful Word.

Why does gravity still work after thousands of years? Because Jesus is speaking it. He's speaking to the earth. Why don't the seas completely overrun dry land? Why doesn't the earth go back to its original form before God spoke to it? Why does it not go back to being *"without form and void"*? Because Jesus is continuing to speak to it.

He's maintaining what He created *with the power of His Words.*

Why don't the stars fall out of the sky? Astronomers think they know, but the Bible says that it's really because Jesus is still speaking to them. He's maintaining what He created by the power of His word. Many Christians are just now learning the power of their spoken word. They're saying, "I spoke this, and it happened. Isn't that great?" But then there are Christians, many who have been at it for a while, who have become good at speaking and seeing things happen, but are not good at *maintaining* or *sustaining* them. It's like, once their checkbook balance gets above zero, they stop speaking to it.

Think of it this way—you get to the point where you need $189.30 to pay your electric bill, so you speak to it. And when the money comes in, you say, "Wow. It was a miracle." But then, you stop speaking to your finances, forgetting the fact that you need to maintain your everyday life by the power of your words.

Don't get bored with the power of your words. Don't get bored with declaring your faith. Don't get bored with hearing messages about the power of your words, because death and life are in them. Too many Christians think it's funny to make jokes about circumstances. "We're going to go on a picnic, but it always rains when we go on a picnic, hahaha. Better take your raincoat and an umbrella!" But be careful, because you're creating an atmosphere around yourself. Of course, not everything you say comes to pass instantaneously. If you say, "Wow, that scared me to death," you're probably not going to fall dead right then, but you are creating an atmosphere of death around you. You may wonder, "Why is everything around me drying up?"

It could be the power of your words.

Why do words work? Let's look at the Book of Romans, remembering that faith is the foundation for everything else on which we're going to build our lives and make them failure proof.

In fact, you may not know this, but faith has a language. What does it say? We learn about this in Romans 10:6, which says, *"But the righteousness of faith speaks in this way. Do not say in your heart, 'who will ascend into heaven,' that is to bring Christ down from above, or 'who will descend into the abyss that is to bring Christ up from the earth. But what does faith say?"*

Many of us have the mindset that if we could just get Jesus to show up on the scene, He'd fix it. We say, "If Jesus were just here, I wouldn't be so sick in my body. If Jesus would just come down from heaven and come into my hospital room and touch me, He could heal me. My finances are such a mess. But if Jesus could just show up on the scene, I know He would fix it."

But Paul was stating that's not what faith says. Faith doesn't say, "Can we get Jesus to come and fix it?" Faith says, in Romans 10:8, that *"the word is near you, in your mouth and in your heart. That is, the word of faith which we preach."* That's what faith says. Faith does not say, "Can I get Jesus to show up and fix this?" Faith says Jesus ascended into heaven and is seated at the Father's right hand. And the same Holy Spirit that brooded over the earth in Genesis chapter one is with us now. But again, nothing's going to happen unless someone speaks. It's our responsibility to take dominion over our

14

circumstances and speak the Word of God over them and see the will of God come to pass in our lives.

Now please don't misunderstand me. We're not leaving Jesus out. Jesus is still present in the power of the Holy Spirit, and He's still present in His Word. John chapter one teaches us that Jesus is in His Word. Jesus is at the right hand of the Father, interceding for us and speaking over what He has created, but it's our responsibility to speak the word of God over our lives and to see the Word of God come to pass. So, the reason words work is because faith has a language. Faith has a voice.

Faith speaks.

How do you know if you have faith? By what comes out of your mouth. We hear people saying, "You know, I'm just believing God for this job. I'm just believing God that my health is going to get better. I'm just believing God that my marriage is going to be better." You don't get it because you believe it. You get it *because you speak it*; you get it because you speak what you believe. It's not enough to believe it. You have to say it. So how do we know we have faith? We know because of what we say. Mark 11:23 tells us that if we *declare* to the mountain to be removed and be cast into the sea, and don't doubt in our hearts but believe that what we *say* will come to pass, we will have whatever we *say*...not just what we believe!

THREE

"Use Your Words"

God called Abram out of his homeland. He said, "I'm going to give you a land. It will belong to you and your children and your children's children and your descendants forever and ever. Abram replied, "But I have no children." And God said, "I will take care of that."

Twenty-five years went by, and Abram still didn't have any children. But in Romans 4:16-17 we read, *"Therefore, it is of faith that it might be according to grace, so that the promise might be sure to all the seed, not only to those who are of the law, but also to those who are of the faith of Abraham, who is the father of us all. (as it is written, 'I have made you a father of many nations') in the presence of Him whom he believed—God who gives life to the dead and calls those things which do not exist as though they did;"* This is what God does. He calls those things that don't exist *as though they do.*

Abram had no children, but as we shall soon see, God referred to Abram as the Father of many nations. He became the Father of many nations, according to what was spoken. According to what? According to what was spoken by God Himself, Abram became the father of many nations. *"So shall your descendants be. Abraham became the Father of many nations."*

At this point, nearly a quarter of a century has passed, and Abram still doesn't have a child. Then, in Genesis 17:1, when Abram was 99 years old, we learn that the Lord appears to him and says, *"I am almighty God. Walk before Me and be blameless. And I will make my covenant between me and you, and I will multiply you exceedingly."* And Abram says, "But you've been telling me that for years." Then Abram fell on his face, and God talked with him, saying, *"As for me, behold, my covenant is with you, and you shall be the father of many nations. No longer shall your name be called Abram, but you shall be called Abraham; for I have made you a father of many nations."* The name that Abram's parents gave him meant "exalted father," but when God changed Abram's name to Abraham, instead of calling himself exalted Father, he began to call himself the Father of a multitude every time he spoke his own name.

No doubt there were those around him who said, "You're nearly one hundred years old, and you have no children!" Nothing seemed to be happening, but when Abraham began to speak over himself, speaking what God was speaking, and when he and God got into agreement, guess what? His 90-year-old wife got pregnant. A hundred-year-old man and a 90-year-old woman had a baby from what they spoke.

They agreed with God with the power of their words, and their words came to pass!

I'm not trying to take God out of the equation, but so many of us are waiting on God. "Why won't God? When is God going to do it? I'm waiting on God. I'm just believing God; one day, He's going to do this."

We're waiting on God, but God's waiting on us.

God waited on Abraham to get in sync with him. The Bible says Abraham believed God, and it was counted to him for righteousness. Abraham believed God for 24 years, yet it still didn't happen. It didn't happen until finally, God said, "How can I get Abraham to get in agreement with me? I know. I'll change his name; then he'll have to say it!"

God changed his name to "father of a multitude." And once he changed his name to "father of a multitude," guess what? Things began to happen. They began to change. That's what will make the difference for you. God is speaking the Word over you and maintaining what He created by the word of his power. Many of you are believing God for what he has for you, and still, nothing's happening. But you don't get it because you believe it. You get it *because you say it*.

"I am blessed. I have that job in Jesus' name. It's mine!"

God will never say, "You can't have that job. You're not qualified for that job. You're not smart enough. You'll never have that much of my money. You'll never have that kind of ministry." You can't keep listening to that negative talk and meditating on it. You have to counterbalance it with the Word. You need to watch what people speak over you and what they say. You need to watch what you meditate on and what comes out of your mouth. So many of us are waiting on God. "When is God going to do this? God, when are you going to show up?" But God's been on the scene the whole time.

He is looking for us to come into agreement with Him.

It says in Romans 4:17, "*that God calls into being things that are not.*" In Mark 11:22, Jesus said, *"Have faith in God."* Many Bibles have a study note in the margin that says, "have the faith of God" or "have the God kind of faith."

Of course, I'm not saying we're all *gods.* Not at all. I'm saying that God wants us to have His kind of faith. If we have the kind of faith He has, then our faith speaks. Look again at what it says in Mark 11:23: *"For assuredly, I say to you, whoever says to this mountain, 'Be removed and be cast into the sea', and does not doubt in his heart, but believes that those things he says will be done, he will have whatever he says."* We need to believe that. We need to exercise our faith, believe God, starve our doubts, and feed our faith with the word of God.

Then we must speak the word.

You see, at times, we put our faith in the wrong place. Notice that Mark 11:23 doesn't say that we need to believe that the mountain will move. Often, we say, "I want the mountain to move. I don't see the mountain moving." We're speaking to the mountain, and we're wrapped up in whether or not we believe that the mountain is going to move. That's not what that verse says. It says, "If you believe that what you say will come to pass, the mountain will move."

Sometimes we put the cart before the horse.

Do you believe that what you say will come to pass? That's the vital question. It's not, "Do you believe the mountain will move?" That's a byproduct of believing that what you say will come to pass. Do you believe that what you say will come to pass? Because, if you do, the mountain will move as a result of speaking what you believe.

What do you believe about what God says about the power of your words? As we saw at the beginning of chapter one, Proverbs 18:21 says, *"Death and life are in the power of the tongue."* The Message paraphrase says that our words are either poison or fruit.

We choose.

Do you believe that? Many of you likely don't. How do I know you don't believe it? Listen to yourself talk. Ask your spouse, "Honey, does the way I talk sound like I believe that I'm going to have what I say?" What would they tell you? Don't ask unless you really want to know.

You may not like their answer.

We are not born with the inclination to speak the Word of God and speak what these verses say. We have to teach our mouths what to say. Just like we need to teach our children to clean their rooms—there's a difference between knowledge and action. Many of our mouths are rebellious. There's a difference between our children knowing how to clean their rooms and them being motivated to clean it. Sure, some of us know the right thing to say, but knowing the right thing to say is not enough. We have to actually speak it. And some of us need to discipline our mouths.

What do you do when you tell Johnny to clean his room and he says, "No"? You have to correct him in love. If you're going to raise an obedient child, you have to discipline him. Some of us need to control our mouths and train them to speak because our mouths are as undisciplined as a child, and they say the first thing that comes to mind. I don't know about you, but most of the time the first thing that comes to my mind is wrong and shouldn't be spoken out of my mouth. I have to *teach* my mouth what to say.

When you don't know what to say, don't say anything until you find the right words. Don't let the devil, people, or circumstances pressure you into speaking something—instead, wait, go to your Bible and study what it has to say about your situation, and speak that. Speak the Word of God, speak the word of faith, and side with God. "Why won't my finances turn around? What's wrong with God?" God's been speaking over your finances for years. God's been speaking over your harvest. You can believe you get a harvest.

But you won't get it until you say it.

FOUR

"One Day"

"Indeed, we put bits in horses' mouths that they may obey us, and we turn their whole body. Look also at ships: although they are so large and are driven by fierce winds, they are turned by a very small rudder wherever the pilot desires. Even so the tongue is a little member and boasts great things." —James 3:3-5 (NKJV)

Have you ever seen a horse's bit? I am not a horse person, but my wife grew up on a farm and loves horses. We even went horseback riding on our first date. But my knowledge about horses is lacking. So, as is the case so often when we need information, I went to the internet. The average thoroughbred quarter horse weighs between 750 and 1,250 pounds. In other words, the average weight is 1,000 pounds—a half-ton.

A bit weighs less than one 1,000th the horse's weight. Yet this tiny bit determines the direction in which that horse will move. You can turn the horse any way you please. When the bit is attached to the harness and is in the horse's mouth, you have complete control of that horse.

Now, imagine if you got on a horse without a saddle. No bit. No Bridle. My wife could do that. I found out when we were dating that she rode really well. But most of us wouldn't be able to control that horse. Where will the horse go? We wouldn't know. We would be destined to wander around at the horse's will.

Scripture next tells us to look at a *rudder*. A *Bayliner* speed boat weighs about 2,800 pounds. The rudder that steers and directs that same boat weighs 17 pounds—less than one percent the weight of the boat. Yet, the rudder determines the 2,800-pound boat's direction! You can have the most powerful engine on that boat, and you can take that boat down the lake at high speed, but without a rudder, you have no control over its direction.

The average human tongue weighs less than an ounce. James says, *"Even so the tongue is a little member and boasts great things."* Just like the bit or the rudder, your tongue is going to determine the direction of your life.

The Message paraphrase says it this way: *"A word out of your mouth may seem of no account, but it can accomplish nearly anything—or destroy it!"* When we talk about the impact of our words, we are not necessarily talking about the power in our life, but the *direction* of our life. Where is your life headed? Are you happy with it? Do you *really* feel like you're headed in the right direction?

Words. They got you into this...they can get you out! You have no direction if you launch that boat, leave the dock, and head across the lake with no rudder. Whatever direction your life is headed in is the sum total of what you have been speaking over your life all these years.

We need to see our lives as precious—like pieces of gold. Yet we waste our worth because we don't have any direction. We don't know where we're really going. We are members of the Body of Christ, but we have no direction! We don't know what God wants us to do with our lives, and often our lives lack meaning.

Why does this happen?

It happens because of the power of the words you are or are not speaking. When people get a revelation of the power of words, so many people in the Body of Christ become afraid of them. They don't say anything because they fear saying the wrong thing. So, they stay stuck and directionless.

If your life has no direction, what should you do to speak the Word of God and propel your life in the direction that God wants for you? If the rudder is guiding a boat headed at high speed in the wrong direction, then there will be serious consequences. It is essential to control your tongue *now*!

We can't keep saying that we will do things differently "one day." I will overcome this addiction one day. I will lose weight one day. I will fix my marriage one day. I will volunteer and give more at church one day. I will take that mission trip to Nicaragua one day. The reality is that you will wake up and realize that you have come to the end of your life and "one day" has come your way over and over.

You just missed it.

I have a friend who skydived for the first time at 81. He was tired of waiting for "one day." We should learn from that;

otherwise, our lives fly by! We are on the lake of life, going full speed, trying to reach a distant shore, with no idea where we are going or how we will get there!

As a pastor, I've spent a lot of time with people nearing the end of their lives, getting ready to meet Jesus. They tell me that they aren't prepared to go, not because they don't know Jesus, but because they didn't do everything God wanted them to do on this earth. And more often than not, people usually look back on their lives and wish they had done things differently, accomplished more, or made more of an impact.

This is about much more than deciding to call the travel agent and take that cruise you've dreamed about...I'm talking about how you use your words. Your words will propel you into your destiny! Your words will determine where you end up in life. What you say with your mouth has everything to do with how you leave this world at the end of your life.

Proverbs 18:21 says, *"Death and life are in the power of the tongue, And those who love it will eat its fruit."* Are you going to experience a life of death? I'm not talking about literal death, but being the *walking dead*—physically alive, but spiritually and emotionally dead. How does that happen? It comes from the power of your words. People walk around physically alive, but with dead marriages, dead finances, or decaying health. And trying harder has nothing to do with it.

You must get control of the rudder of your life.

Don't just drive the boat faster, you will just reach the wrong place more quickly! Set the rudder in the course that God has for your life. Once you have done that, you can go as fast as God allows. But only if that rudder, which is the power of your words, is first set in the right direction.

What words are you speaking over your life? What words are you speaking over your family? Over your business? Sometimes I ask people how they are doing, and they answer back, "Do you want a 'faith answer' or the real answer?" I always want the honest answer. And when the rudder of your life is set in the right direction, the faith answer equals the honest answer. We have to stop setting the rudder based on the circumstances of life and set it instead based on the Word of God.

This spiritual principle always works, but whether or not it works in your favor depends on what you say. So many people just don't understand the power of their words. Jesus aimed His ministry and kept it on track by His words. Jesus is the

Champion of the power of the spoken word. Jesus created the reality of the universe by His own words in Genesis.

In Genesis chapter one, we read that seven times God said, "*Let there be…,*" and creation happened as He *spoke* it! In the Gospel of John 1:1-4, we read that the God of creation was actually Jesus, and He created the world with His words. This truth is reinforced in the Book of Hebrews chapter eleven: *"By faith we understand that the worlds were framed by the word of God."* It was also with the power of His words that He established His earthly ministry.

The Bible says, in Luke 4:1-4, *"Then Jesus, being filled with the Holy Spirit, returned from the Jordan and was led by the Spirit into the wilderness, being tempted for forty days by the devil. And in those days He ate nothing, and afterward, when they had ended, He was hungry. And the devil said to Him, 'If You are the Son of God, command this stone to become bread.' But Jesus answered him, saying, 'It is written, "Man shall not live by bread alone, but by every word of God."'"*

"It is written." That is such an important phrase. As Jesus interacts with the devil, He speaks the Word. This occurred at the beginning of Jesus' ministry, when He was about 30-years-old. His ministry did not begin with miracles but with fasting and prayer in the wilderness. When Jesus became

hungry, the devil attempted to tempt Him, but it quickly became evident that the first 30 years of Jesus' life had been established on the bedrock of the Word of God.

Naturally, His reply to Satan was the Word of God. Jesus didn't whine to His Father about His circumstances. He didn't worry, but He simply spoke the truth of the Word to the enemy. So, the devil tried another angle, and then another. But Jesus centered His life in the Word, so the Word is what came out of His mouth. His ministry wasn't built on a big budget. It wasn't built on a staff of the sharpest ministers from the Temple. It was not built on a big building. His ministry was built on the power of the Words that came from His mouth. And He established the greatest ministry that has ever been on the face of the earth!

He spoke miracles into existence. He spoke to a fig tree, and it died because it did not bear fruit. He spoke, and circumstances changed. That is how Jesus established His life. Before the boat started across the lake of His Ministry, He first set the rudder. Then He launched the boat. We need to learn this, and we need to teach this to our children, too.

We need to understand how to speak the Word of God.

FIVE

"You Are in the Bible"

When I was a young father, my kids didn't understand at first what I was trying to teach them about the power of words. They would skin a knee, or be bleeding, and say, "I think I'm going to die!" I would correct them in love and teach them how to speak words of truth over themselves.

You have to set that rudder when your kids are young. Don't allow your children or your teenagers to walk around your house, saying things that are not according to the Word. If they live in your home, then they need to live and speak a certain way. There are rules that they must follow, after all, like brushing their teeth or going to school. Speaking the

Word should not be optional for them, either. If they can watch cartoons, they can speak the Word.

Kids may sometimes find it hard to understand what is going on in church. It may be over their heads. Yet, my five-year-old granddaughter can log herself onto a computer and start clicking that mouse, knowing exactly how to get to where she wants to go.

She's five.

So, there are no excuses. Jesus aimed His ministry by the power of His Words, and so should we. Luke 4:16-21 says, *"So He came to Nazareth, where He had been brought up. And as His custom was, He went into the Synagogue on the Sabbath day, and stood up to read. And He was handed the book of the prophet Isaiah. And when He had opened the book, He found the place where it was written: 'The Spirit of the Lord is upon Me, because He has anointed Me to preach the gospel to the poor; He has sent Me to heal the brokenhearted, to proclaim liberty to the captives and recovery of sight to the blind, to set at liberty those who are oppressed; To proclaim the acceptable year of the Lord.' Then He closed the book, and gave it back to the attendant and sat down. And the eyes of all who were in the Synagogue were fixed on Him. And He began to say to them, 'Today this Scripture is fulfilled in your hearing.'"*

Jesus turned to Isaiah chapter 61, and said, "That's me!" Have you ever found yourself in the Bible? Did you know that you are in the Bible? Deuteronomy 28 says that you are blessed when you come in, and when you go out! Gal. 6:7 tells us not to be deceived. God is not mocked. Whatever you sow, you will reap. If you're a sower, then you are in the Bible. Jeremiah, in chapter 29, talks about God having plans for our future. You are in that promise. God has a future for you.

You are in the Bible!

Jesus found Himself in the Bible, and He set the rudder of His ministry by opening scripture and saying, "This is who I am and what I am here to accomplish on earth." He set that rudder and held onto the power of His tongue. And so can we, because nobody can stop the power of your tongue if you keep the rudder set just like Jesus did. Jesus has given you more power than the devil has to stop you through the power of your words. More power than any person has to stop you.

People can't keep you from your destiny. Only you can keep you from your destiny. The devil cannot stop you from what God has for you. Only you can get discouraged, and quit and miss your destiny.

A while back, my wife and I were out on the lake with some friends. I was steering the boat, and it was not easy that day because I kept having to avoid obstacles in the water. Those who have driven boats know that even a small branch or piece of driftwood floating on the lake can be dangerous. You have to steer the boat around the debris to avoid tangling it in the propeller or the rudder. But don't let it stop you. In the same way, you will sometimes need to steer your life around and away from people and circumstances that have become obstacles to God's Will in your life.

After Jesus preached in the Synagogue, and He had sat down, the people became angry. Luke 4:28-29 says, *"So all those in the synagogue, when they heard these things, were filled with wrath, and rose up and thrust Him out of the city; and they led Him to the brow of the hill on which their city was built, that they might throw Him down over the cliff."*

The people in the Synagogue were angry that Jesus knew His destiny and they didn't. They were threatened because Jesus found Himself in the Bible, and they didn't.

Why do people get irritated when you have a destiny, and they don't? People may get intimidated by you. Maybe it feels threatening to be around someone who knows who they are and where they are going. These people were undoubtedly intimidated by Jesus.

So, find yourself in the Bible, but don't let others intimidate you. Anytime you read scripture, if you see the word, "you," guess what? It's talking to *you*. You are in the Bible. And Jesus found His destiny in the Word, which made the people so angry that they were going to throw Him off a cliff! But then verse 30: *"Then passing through the midst of them, He went His way."*

This is one of the most powerful verses in Scripture.

Jesus' rudder was set; Jesus had spoken the power of the Word. He had revealed His destiny, found in Scripture, to the people. He was to heal the broken hearted and free the captives. And the mob was trying to stop Him.

Too many people, when confronted by others, give up on their destiny because they haven't firmly set their rudder. Ask yourself, what am I doing here? Why am I at this church? What is it that God is calling me to do? Who should I marry? Why am I married to the person that I'm married to? Why did God give me the children that I have? Why do I have the job that I hold? Why?

Because there is purpose in all of it. What is that purpose? That purpose is discovered by studying the Word and then speaking it aloud. You need to say it, spray it, slice it, and dice it. It needs to become a part of you, to the point that your rudder is firmly set.

The mob could not throw Jesus off the cliff because He was called by God to be there. We can have that assurance too. The mob can't throw you off the cliff because God has called you to something in your life, and you are speaking the Word over it, and your rudder is set. And nobody, even the devil, will keep you from doing what God has called you to do.

But what happens when we don't speak? I'm not just talking about task list items that we must complete to be spiritually fit. I am talking about the power of your words and what you say. If your words and your task list are leading you in opposite directions, you will go in the direction of your words every time. So, if your words and your task list match, you have a winning combination! But too often, we make a task list that is based on our own desires. It didn't come from God. We are trying to look like everyone else and do what others are doing.

Ministers are really bad about doing this. They go to a ministry conference to see what other churches are doing, so they can change. What happens so often, however, is that we pick up on the latest Church growth "fad" that the Holy Spirit never intended for our church. It doesn't really fit our culture, and in the end, it just doesn't work for us.

When it comes to direction, sometimes we assume we are going the right way. But God never gave you that direction, and you are only doing it because someone else is doing it. It would be best if you found out why you are unique. God made you for a unique purpose. And if you are trying to be someone else, then who will be *you*?

We must find out what God has called us to do. Then we have to set that rudder, and we must find ourselves constantly in the Word.

What if I have a bad medical report that says I am at high risk for a stroke? I have to believe that I have a divine destiny, and I can't let a stroke keep me from fulfilling it. I have to set the rudder of my life. So, we say this: "In Jesus' name, my body is blessed. I am the temple of the Holy Spirit. I will change what I eat. I will fulfill my destiny."

You won't do your family any good if you don't quit smoking. So say this: "I am the temple of the Holy Spirit. I have a destiny to fulfill, and I refuse to allow my habits to cut my life short. I declare that I have victory over smoking, in Jesus' Name!"

Verse 30 says, *"Then passing through the midst of them, He went His way."* The crowd tried to throw Jesus off a cliff. But Jesus was just getting started in His ministry. He knew His destiny. He spoke His destiny from the Word. So, He simply walked right through the angry crowd and went on with His day.

Can you imagine how intimidating it would be to be forced to the edge of a cliff by an angry mob? They want to push you off, and they are angry and cursing at you and throwing things at you. Are you afraid? Do you fear the impending death?

Not Jesus. He knew that this was not what God had planned for Him. Jesus laid out that plan in the Synagogue. And being thrown from a cliff was not a part of the plan. Jesus had done no miracles yet. He was still setting the rudder based on the Word. So, He walked through the crowd.

Why can't we be like Jesus? Jesus didn't yet have the proof of the Words He spoke, but He never doubted their truth. He hadn't done miracles yet, and Jesus' miracles were a vital part of His ministry. But at this point, He was still setting the rudder, and He knew the power was in the Word.

Verses 31-32 say, *"Then He went down to Capernaum, a city of Galilee, and was teaching them on the Sabbaths. And they were astonished at His teaching, for His word was with authority."*

For three years, the devil tried to get in Jesus' way. He tried to distract Him from His plan. He even had Jesus nailed to a cross. But He couldn't keep Jesus from His destiny because Jesus set His rudder and the direction of His life with the power of the words that He spoke over Himself.

What about the rudder of your life? Is your direction set? Or are you wandering back and forth across the lake? Some of you have been meandering around on the lake of life for a long time, and you don't know where you are going. You are working hard, but you can't work hard enough if your rudder isn't set. If the direction of your life isn't set by your words, no amount of hard work will make up for a lack of direction.

SIX

"So I Started Praying"

What does the Bible say about *you*?

Luke 5:8-11 says, *"When Simon Peter saw it, he fell down at Jesus' knees, saying, 'Depart from me, for I am a sinful man, O Lord!' For he and all who were with him were astonished at the catch of fish which they had taken; and so also were James and John, the sons of Zebedee, who were partners with Simon. And Jesus said to Simon, 'Do not be afraid. From now on you will catch men.' So when they had brought their boats to land, they forsook all and followed Him."*

Simon knew he had shortcomings. He had problems. He had difficulties. He knew he was a sinful man, and he told Jesus so. But Jesus spoke something else. Jesus spoke something utterly different about him. Jesus said that Simon would become a fisher of men.

Jesus spoke over His team, something different than they were speaking over themselves. How often do we speak words of faith about the people around us? Those who are in our environment, who could make a difference in our lives? One of the reasons that many people do not prosper in their jobs is because of what they are saying about their bosses and their companies. They complain. They gossip. And then they wonder why they aren't making more money or why they were passed over for the promotion.

There is a spiritual principle in Matthew chapter 25 that says, *"if you are faithful with little, you can be entrusted with much."* Your faithfulness does not begin with what you do with your hands or on your computer. Your faithfulness begins with your tongue.

I was privileged to lead excellent staff members at the churches I pastored. Working at a church can be challenging. There are many opportunities for frustration, and we really have to watch our words. To stay faithful, we must start with our words, just like Jesus.

Jesus spoke over His team. Simon told Jesus that he was an unclean, sinful man. And Jesus told Him that he would be a fisher of men. We must speak the right things over our coworkers. Over our families. This will make a huge difference. Proverbs 18:21 says, *"Words kill, words give life; they're either poison or fruit—you choose."* (*The Message*)

If you are in an atmosphere of death at your job, take a few moments and reflect how much of your work environment is because you created it with the words of your own mouth.

In Mark chapter three, we see a list of Jesus' disciples. In verse 16, we see that Jesus called Simon, but He changed his name to Peter. Simon was a common name in Biblical times. It was like the name, Bubba, in the South.

Jesus changed his name to Peter—The Rock—and Jesus demonstrated that He was not going to call him what everyone else called him. Jesus called Peter the name that He needed him to be, not what was apparent to the natural eye.

Jesus doesn't call you by your shortcomings. Jesus calls you by what He needs you to be. He calls you strong. He calls you powerful. He calls you loving and kind. He calls you a blessing to others. And we need to see ourselves the same way and speak that truth. More importantly, we need to see others that way and speak the truth over them as well. When we come to the point where we realize how powerful our words are, we will change what we say about others.

I was pastoring a small church of about 60 people several years ago. In small churches, everyone knows everyone else really well. There was one particular lady who had constant emotional problems, and she was dragging everyone else down. Even with her emotional problems, she often wanted to prophesy to everyone else, telling them what they needed to do rather than looking at her own issues. Her own life was a wreck. And this went on for a long time until one day I was fed up with it.

So, I started praying.

I told God that I knew I couldn't pray this lady out of the church, and He told me that, actually, I could. He said, "You're the pastor, so if you ask, I will remove her."

I felt guilty about that. I asked Him, "Is this what I should do?" The Lord asked me "What have you been saying about her?" I answered, "Well, she's a gossip. And a flake." Along with several other things. He said to me, "Could that be one of the reasons that she is like she is? *You don't understand the power of your words!*"

I decided right then I would teach my mouth what to say about her. I changed my declaration that day. I said, "In Jesus' name, I pray that she will come to her senses and escape the path the devil has laid out for her. I say that she has the mind of Christ and the thoughts, feelings, and purposes of His heart. I say that she is emotionally stable."

Two days later, she called me, blubbering like a baby. She just kept saying, "I'm sorry for this. I'm sorry for that. I don't know what got into me."

She snapped out of it, just like that!

Of course, not everyone changes when we pray for them or speak the Word over them, because their will is involved. But let's be sure that the issues that people are dealing with aren't because of what WE declared over them!

Peter protested to Jesus that he was an unclean man. And Jesus had every right to say, "Yeah, you are right. You are too much of a hothead. You're pretty rough. You have a big mouth that gets you in trouble."

But instead, Jesus called Peter a fisher of men. Then Jesus confessed with His mouth that Peter would be the rock upon which He would build His church. Jesus chose to speak the right things over Peter, even in the courtyard when Peter denied that he even knew Jesus. Jesus already knew what Peter would do. He predicted that before the rooster crowed three times, Peter would deny Him.

Peter emphatically said that He would never do that. Yet it is exactly what happened. But when Jesus rose from the dead, He told Mary to tell His disciples, and specifically Peter, that He was alive. He knew that Peter would be feeling extreme guilt and despair over his denial of Christ at the time of His death.

Jesus was still speaking the right thing over Peter, even when Peter betrayed Him!.

What are you speaking over the people in your life? What about your work environment? Is your boss a jerk because you said he was? Is your company losing money because you said it would? How much of your environment has been created by your words?

"Death and life are in the power of your tongue. And those who love it will eat its fruit." —Proverbs 18:21 (NKJV)

"Words kill, words give life; they're either poison or fruit—you choose." —Proverbs 18:21 (The Message)

SEVEN

"Hush, Hush"

There is a wonderful illustration recorded in the fourth chapter of the Gospel of Mark about the storms in our lives and speaking the Word of God.

One of my great concerns is that the messages that we preach and teach are not mere entertainment or religious exercises, but rather a way to have hearers leave knowing they can accomplish great things. When you go to a concert, to a ballet, or to a show, you sit and watch. The talent is amazing. Sometimes people watch shows, and there's a piece of it that they find themselves connecting to vicariously. That's why some people play air guitars. They imagine they are their own guitar hero—whoever that is. I never want the people of my congregation to leave a service thinking, "Oh, that's so cool," yet fail to believe in their hearts what God is saying about them.

One of the challenges I have as a preacher of the gospel is helping people understand this stuff is not just good preaching material. Sure, sometimes it's entertaining, even fun, and that's great, but it's never to be just that. When Jesus taught his disciples, He did not tell them, "Don't try this at home." It was designed for us to put into practice every day.

Mark 4:35 says, *"On the same day when evening had come, Jesus said to his disciples, let us cross over to the other side."* When they left the multitude, the disciples took Jesus along with them in the boat to cross the Sea of Galilee. Other boats were with Him, and a great windstorm arose. The waves beat into the ship. It was quickly filling with water and in danger of capsizing.

It was a serious situation.

Have you ever been in a storm? I mean a real storm, not one like, "My mommy wouldn't let me float my boats in the bathtub, and now I've grown up, and I'm disillusioned about life." I'm not talking about that. I'm talking about the devil trying to destroy your marriage, finances, or health. I'm talking about an onslaught from hell.

The Amplified Bible says, *"a great windstorm arose, and the waves beat into the boat."* This windstorm was of hurricane proportions. Can you imagine? Yet, Jesus is in the stern of the ship asleep on a pillow.

They woke him and said, *"'Teacher, do you not care that we are perishing?' And he arose. And he rebuked the wind and said to the sea, 'peace, be still!', and the wind ceased. And there was a great calm. And he said to them, 'why are you so fearful? How is it that you have no faith?' And they feared extremely and said to one another, 'who can this be? That even the wind and the sea obey him.'"*

Jesus was asleep.

I have a theory, and it's dangerous to come up with theories about Scripture, but I don't think Jesus was asleep. I believe He was playing "possum." I think Mark thought Jesus was asleep, and I believe He looked as though He was sleeping on purpose. Think about it. Jesus was in a boat, in a hurricane, and He was sleeping. He was not worried. He was not stressed. I think Jesus was at peace, but I'm not sure He was asleep. I think Jesus wanted to see what the disciples were going to do. He heard everything they were saying. "I'm not waking Him up. *You* wake Him up. Remember the last time we woke Him up? I'm not waking Him up. You wake Him, not me." Jesus was hearing all of this, and He wanted to watch how they were going to react to this dire situation.

So, they woke Him.

Jesus stood in the stern of the boat and said to the storm, *"Peace, be still."* The Amplified Bible says, *"Hush, hush."* Jesus did not have a prayer meeting with his disciples. He didn't say, "Let's all kneel in the boat here and pray. Peter, why don't you lead off? Dear God, our Father in heaven, would you please help us? We're about to drown here."

No, He spoke to the storm.

Many of you have storms in your life. Your finances are in a whirlwind, your marriage is in a hurricane. Your health is going down the tubes and you're saying, "Oh God, please. Somehow in your omnipotence, would you stop the storm, please?"

God does not listen to us because we're religious or because we pray for a long time. Let me give you the revised "Caronna translation" of these verses in Mark. Jesus says, "Why didn't you do this? You woke me up for this? Where's your faith? I've been working hard to heal the sick and raise the dead, cast out devils, and preach. I was tired. I needed some sleep, and you woke me up for this?"

Sometimes God is saying the same thing to us. God loves us. The Bible says He watches over Israel and neither slumbers nor sleeps. He's watching over us, and He cares for us. God doesn't get irritated because we need Him, but He has given us authority over things, and we need to take dominion.

We need to speak into our situation. Mark. 4:38-40, in *The Message* translation, says, *"They roused him, saying, 'Teacher, is it nothing to you that we're going down? Awake now,' he told the wind to pipe down and said to the sea, 'Quiet! Settle down!' The wind ran out of breath; the sea became smooth as glass. Jesus reprimanded the disciples: 'Why are you such cowards? Don't you have any faith at all?'"*

The Amplified Bible said the sea became perfect peacefulness. Wouldn't you love to have perfect peacefulness in your finances? How about in your marriage? How about in your work environment? Wouldn't you like to have perfect peacefulness? Unfortunately, you're not going to have it until you *speak* it.

Jesus reprimanded the disciples. "Why are you such cowards? Don't you have any faith at all?" They were in absolute awe. Who is this guy?

Listen to me very carefully. When you're going through the storm, don't stay away from church. Don't stay away from your Christian friends. Don't stay away from the people who brought you along in faith. That's the very time you need them. When you're going through a storm, when you're going through difficulty, that's the very time you need them the most.

Years ago, my wife Connie and I went through a difficult season. I will tell you that I know what it's like to not want to go to church. I do. I know what it's like for my life to be such a mess. I think, "I'm afraid if I go to church, I'll crack. I'm afraid I'll break out crying. If I go to church, I'm afraid somebody's going to find out that I'm dealing with this, and I'm dealing with that. I've got so many problems."

Christian friends would ask me, "How are you doing?" I'd reply, "Fine. I'm fine. Everything's fine."

There's a difference between a positive declaration and a coverup. If you're fine because you're standing on the Word, that's wonderful. But if you're saying "fine" because you're hiding, that's not fine at all. We need to open up to people of faith around us so that they can challenge us. Stand on the Word even when you feel rotten. Stand on the Word, even when everything's falling apart. Stand on the Word. Keep speaking the Word, keep believing the Word. Never let go of the Word.

One question I've wanted to ask someone who had experienced healing, but never asked them, was, "Did you have any opposition?" Do you have people in your life that when you told them, "I'm the healed of the Lord," they just said, "You're in denial?" You need to know the difference. There is, of course, such a thing as denial, don't get me wrong. There are people who are in denial. Instead of speaking to their circumstances, they deny that they even have them. That's not faith, that's foolishness.

Sometimes your confidence will look like you're uncaring or overconfident to others. Jesus is asleep in your boat, there's a storm going on, yet you're at peace. You can sleep. Other people will think you don't care. Some people will think you're overconfident. I believe God that when I pray for the people of my congregation and when I speak the Word for them, I believe they're well. Absolutely. When I pray for them and stand on the Word with them, I believe that they are well, right then.

What do you believe? The Bible says, "where two or more agree," not "just when the pastor prays." I'm going to do my part, but you need to do your part, which is to stand on the Word, speak the Word, and believe God for His Word to come to pass in your life. That's what you have to believe.

One other thing I need to point out is in Mark 4:36. This passage says that when they left the multitude and got into the boat, the storm came up. So often, when you leave the multitude of the saints and you're out on your own, that's when the storms come up.

When you get out from under the protection of the covering God has for you, that's when storms come. So, stay hooked in and close to those you know are close to God. Do you have Christian friends that challenge you? Friends that, if you're not speaking the Word, will get in your face? Everybody needs some friends like that. I have one that lives with me. I so appreciate my wife Connie's gentle reminders (most of the time!) that I need to continually speak words of faith.

You need to stay tight with people of faith.

EIGHT

"This is for Everyone"

If you're new to faith, you may not be aware that there are people who are very much opposed to the concept of the power of words. They don't comprehend the power of their words. They don't realize words contain the power of life and death. They laugh at those who believe as we do and may even call us names. I understand some take this doctrine too far, as with anything else in Scripture, but what I'm teaching is true. You can search the internet and find books against what I'm telling you. You can turn on television preachers, and I believe many of them are doing a great job, but some of the programs have questionable doctrine. Even some on Christian radio will falsely tell you that your words have no power.

The Bible teaches directly the opposite.

In I Corinthians 1:10, the apostle Paul says, *"Now I plead with you brethren by the name of our Lord Jesus Christ, that you all speak the same thing, that there be no divisions among you, but that you be perfectly joined together in the same mind and the same judgment."*

When you attend church on Sunday, you may think, "I like the music, and my children like the children's program. I really liked the message on prayer from a couple of weeks ago, and I'm going to pray, but when it comes to the message from the preacher on making faith declarations, I can take it or leave it. So, I probably won't do that."

But Paul said, "I'm pleading with you in the name of the Lord, Jesus Christ; I want all of you to do what he says." He said, "I want you all to speak the same thing." What is he talking about? Does he mean he wants me to find out what you're saying, and say the same thing that you're saying? Does he mean that he wants you to follow me around and repeat what I'm saying during the day?

Actually, no.

Paul wants us to be perfectly joined together in the same mind and the same judgment. How does that all happen? If we're all speaking the word of God, then those words will create environments around us, where we are together in agreement, and we keep division out. If you're in a difficult situation and your marriage, finances, and health, are a mess, or if you're depressed, your words got you into that, and your words can get you out. That's what the Bible teaches. Paul says this is for everybody, not just for two or three. This is not just for the "name it and claim it" crowd.

This is for everyone.

I want to be in a church where if I have health challenges, I have a church full of people who are going to speak the same thing, which is not, "He'll be dead any day," but instead, "He is healed. By the stripes of Jesus, he was healed!"

Can you imagine how much power a church would have if everybody would get in agreement and speak the same thing? No one would say, "Oh, they'll never get that building built. That'll always just be a big hole in the ground. They're never going to get that thing done." Instead, we would be able to build whatever we needed, and be able to reach so many more people, if the church could just get in agreement with her words.

For example, some people left my congregation when we moved into a new building. They said, "They'll never be able to afford a million and a half dollar piece of property, right on a major highway and then pay two million to renovate it. They'll never do that." But we did it, by walking in agreement and, as Paul instructed us, we all *spoke* the same thing together.

It's not that we were more intelligent than everybody else, or that God loves us more. But we got what we said we would in Jesus' Name. When we ran out of parking space and needed to build a new parking lot, we said, "It's ours in His Name. We're going to possess it in Jesus' name. We're going to build a parking lot that will be paid for by the time it's built. We're going to build a parking lot with excellence, and we're going to do it under budget."

We spoke it.

We went out to our property, walked the land, and even talked to the dirt on the land when there wasn't a bank in town that wanted to talk to us. Thank God for the bank that finally did because we spoke this place into existence, and thank God that we got a line of credit, but we never needed it because of the words that we spoke.

It's not because God loves us any more than He loves anyone else. It's because of this Scripture, where Paul says, "I'm pleading with you as your pastor. I'm pleading with you that if we would all speak the same thing, there would be no divisions among us. That we would speak what the Bible says about the families in our church and about our loved ones that need to be saved."

You may say concerning someone, "Oh, he'll never be saved." Never say that over your children or anyone else's children. "We'll never be able to build that. Oh, they'll never buy that house. They'll never be able to get a car. They'll never be anywhere else or do anything besides what they're doing." You don't want to go to a church like that. You want to go to a church where everybody knows the power of their words and they all speak the same thing, and there are no divisions among them, which is what Paul is saying. He knows that the power of God will be present and in operation in that church.

When many people begin to understand what faith declarations are, they realize they've been speaking negative things over their life for a long time. They want to stop speaking those bad things, so they stop saying anything. Faith declarations are not the same thing as no declaration. You don't get it because you don't say negative things, and you don't get it because you don't say anything, either. You get it because you say what God says in His Word.

You don't stay well because you don't declare sickness. You stay well because you declare healing. Some people decide, "Well, I don't want to say anything bad, so I won't say anything." So, they don't declare anything. Don't do that. You have to stop saying the bad stuff and intentionally say the good stuff. You must be in a church that speaks the same things as you. Paul didn't say, "I'm pleading with you that you all believe the same thing." It's possible to believe something and not get it.

You don't get your harvest just because you believe it. You don't get healing just because you believe it. You don't get delivered from discouragement just because you believe it. You get it because you *say* it. We're not able to accomplish the things that we're able to accomplish as a church just because we believe them; we're able to accomplish them because we say them.

I know churches that say they believe in the gifts of the Spirit but you never see them. I know churches that talk about healing but they haven't had anyone healed in that church in 20 years. They believe it; it's in their doctrinal statement. They believe healing is a part of the atonement. Everybody's trying to find a church that believes what they believe. However, you don't want a church that believes what you believe. You want them to go a step further. You should want a church that speaks the Word of God, and if you're speaking the Word and they're speaking the Word, you're speaking the same thing. That's where the power is.

The power is not in just believing; the power is in speaking.

NINE

"He Did Not Believe God"

In the Book of Exodus chapter 17, we see something really fascinating. *"The whole Israelite community set out from the Desert of Sin, traveling from place to place as the Lord commanded. They camped at Rephidim, but there was no water for the people to drink."* The people got angry at Moses. They started to complain and get upset, crying, "You brought us out here in the wilderness to die!" Moses went before God and said, "God, the people are about to stone me. What do I do?" The Lord answered Moses, "Go out in front of the people. Take with you some of the elders of Israel and take in your hand the staff with which you struck the Nile, and go."

Moses had struck the Red Sea with the rod of God, and the Bible says, *"'I will stand there before you by the rock at Horeb. Strike the rock, and water will come out of it for the people to drink.' So, Moses did so in the sight of the elders of Israel."*

Some time ago, *National Geographic* reported that they found Mount Sinai. It's located in a desert that gets a mere half-inch of rain annually. On the side of the mountain, there is a large split in the rock where it's obvious that water has gushed out. Equally fascinating is that adjacent to this crevice, the stone has been scorched by intense heat.

Exodus 17:6 says, *"I will stand there before you by the rock at Horeb."* So clearly, this is the place where the pillar of God stood. I know for some of you, that's a stretch for you to believe because *National Geographic* found it, and they're evolutionists, but that doesn't change the fact it is where God stood. It's very powerful to me that they found the real Mount Sinai.

At the time of this story in Exodus 17, there were more than three million Israelites, plus all their livestock. We're not talking about a small basin of water being provided. When Moses hit that rock, there was enough water for three million people and all their livestock.

68

Jumping over to Numbers 20:2, the Israelites have traveled farther into the wilderness and again there was no water for the congregation. So, the Israelites gathered together against Moses and Aaron. Again, Moses went before God, asking, "Why did you bring us out here in the wilderness? We're going to die. Our livestock is going to die."

In verse six, Scripture tells us, *"Moses and Aaron went from the assembly to the entrance to the tent of meeting and fell facedown, and the glory of the Lord appeared to them. The Lord said to Moses, 'Take the staff, and you and your brother Aaron gather the assembly together. Speak to that rock before their eyes and it will pour out its water. You will bring water out of the rock for the community so they and their livestock can drink.' So, Moses took the staff from the Lord's presence, just as he commanded him."*

Now they were in the same situation as before. They were near the rock, and Moses was ready to strike it as before, but God said, "I don't want you to hit it. I want you to talk to it. And I want you to say, 'Water, come forth.'" Moses and Aaron gathered the assembly together before the rock and Moses said to them, *"'Listen, you rebels, must we bring you water out of this rock?' Then Moses raised his arm and struck the rock twice with his staff. Water gushed out, and the community and their livestock drank."*

Moses was irritated with the children of Israel because of their complaints. Rather than speak to the rock as God instructed, Moses lifted his hand and struck the rock twice with his rod and water came out of it—abundantly. The congregation and their animals drank. The people rejoiced.

But God was not happy.

If it had only been Moses and Aaron at work, there probably wouldn't have been water coming from the rock. Moses and Aaron would likely have died of thirst alongside the rest of the children of Israel because God was very angry with Moses. But water did come out of the rock because God had compassion and provided water for the people.

> *"Then the Lord spoke to Moses and Aaron and said, 'because you did not believe me to hallow me in the eyes of the children of Israel. Therefore you shall not bring this assembly into the land, which I have given them.'"*

In other words, you've come this far in the desert, but you are not going into the Promised Land because of your disobedience in striking the rock.

What does this tell us? First of all, God was angry with Moses because of his unbelief. God told Moses, *"The first time I said, if you hit that rock with the rod of God, water would come out of it. The second time, if you'll only speak to it, water will come out."* Moses did not believe that would happen.

He did not believe God.

Of course, we know Moses was angry with the children of Israel, and I've often even heard preachers say that Moses hit the rock because of that anger. However, that's not what this passage says. God said, "You didn't believe me. I told you to speak to it and you didn't believe me. Therefore, you are not going into the Promised Land." Many people do not believe that what they speak will come to pass. But in Mark 11: 23-24, Jesus said:

> *"For assuredly, I say to you, whoever says to this mountain, 'Be removed and be cast into the sea,' and does not doubt in his heart, but believes that those things he says will be done, he will have whatever he says. Therefore I say to you, whatever things you ask when you pray, believe that you receive them, and you will have them..."*

That is the same power we should have seen in this story in the Book of Numbers. Moses had a perfect opportunity to demonstrate to three million people how the power of words works, but instead acted in doubt and rebellion.

Do you believe that what you say will come to pass and that you will have whatever you say? God told Moses he couldn't enter into the Promised Land because of his unbelief. Likewise, many of us are not entering our own Promised Land because we don't believe what we say will come to pass. But the Bible says we will have what we say.

Moses didn't believe God when He said, "Speak to the rock. Water will come out of it." Instead, he said, "I remember the time I hit the rock with the rod of God. Water came out; let's do it that way." He hit the rock with the rod of God, and he didn't speak to it. Yes, water came out of it, but it cost him the Promised Land. What will the cost be for you? I've found it's easy to say the right things at church. But it's when you're in the fight of your life that you find out what's really in your mouth.

1 Corinthians 10:1 tells us, *"For I do not want you to be ignorant of the fact, brothers and sisters, that our ancestors were all under the cloud and that they all passed through the sea. They were all baptized into Moses in the cloud and in the sea. They all ate the same spiritual food and drank the same spiritual drink; for they*

drank from the spiritual rock that accompanied them, and that rock was Christ."

The word Christ, in this passage, does not refer to the person of Jesus or the Lordship of Jesus. It's a reference to the *anointing* of Jesus. Christ means the "anointed one," and the anointing that is with Him. It's His anointing. So when it says, "That rock was Christ," it means the anointing of God to remove burdens and destroy the yokes of bondage from the enemy.

In Numbers chapter 20, we are told that Moses lifted his hand, struck the rock twice with the rod, and water came out. However, God had told him to speak to the rock. What are you striving to accomplish on your own that actually requires the anointing of God to accomplish? Instead, we take the rod, and we beat the rock. Do you have something you're trying to make happen in your life? In order to get the anointing and power of God to move in your situation, you have to speak to it.

So many people are waiting for God to do something to miraculously deliver them from their financial problems or their marriage difficulties. They cry out, "God, would you please do something in my husband? Would you please do something with my children? God, would you do something in my body? I've got health problems." They're waiting for God to do something because they don't recognize that what moves the anointing of God is when they speak His Word.

The problem with that is it's not spectacular. We like spectacular things. We like when people experience miraculous healings and miracles. But the power of God is not always moving like that. Sometimes it can just be a show. So many Christians love a good show.

But when we are declaring God's Word over our lives, our marriages, our health, and our finances, it so often is a progression rather than immediate results. We gradually begin to see small changes that, if we are patient, and continue to speak the Word, we will eventually begin to grow into God's Perfect Plan!

TEN

"Grownups Feed Themselves"

Hollywood does the spectacular really well—so does Las Vegas. They've got some great shows. You can hear Celine Dion; her show is a spectacular production with all its lights and glamour. And Christians want the spectacular in church as well. We want to see amazing things happen. But we don't realize that when the anointing of God is moving, and people are speaking forth the will of God and the Word of God, God is then moving in our midst in power.

That's the challenge with so much effective ministry; some of it is just not spectacular. This is where we get messed up. Like Moses, we keep striking the rock, trying to get something to happen, trying to get people worked up into a frenzy rather than just speaking to the rock and seeing the miraculous happen because we're speaking to situations in faith.

In 1 Corinthians 2:1, Paul talked about the anointing and the power of God related to our speech. *"And so it was with me, brothers and sisters. When I came to you, I did not come with eloquence or human wisdom as I proclaimed to you the testimony about God. For I resolved to know nothing while I was with you except Jesus Christ and him crucified. I came to you in weakness with great fear and trembling. My message and my preaching were not with wise and persuasive words, but with a demonstration of the Spirit's power, so that your faith might not rest on human wisdom, but on God's power."*

I've heard people use this Scripture to justify the fact that we don't really need powerful preaching and teaching, but rather what we need are a lot of miracles. Now, thank God for miracles. But how many of you know that miracles are primarily to reach people outside of the Kingdom of God with the power of the gospel?

Miracles are not mainly for Christians—they're for the lost. We need to graduate from desiring miracles to speaking the Word and seeing the Word of God come to pass in our lives.

I'm not teaching against miracles. We've had them happen in our congregation. Once there was a little girl in my congregation, about five years old, who was born deaf in one ear. In a prayer service, we prayed for her, and the ear opened. Thank God for miracles like hers. But the thing I'm trying to get you to see is that, once you grow to a certain level in your faith, you don't keep waiting on a miracle. You start declaring the Word of God and allowing it to produce miracles in your life.

Another member of my congregation, named Elaine, prayed just once over the cancer diagnosis she had received. She said, "I prayed, and I decided I was going to stand on the Word of God. I went back to the doctor, and it was worse. I went to another doctor and, again, it was worse. Over and over my condition worsened. So, what did I do? I stood on the Word. And as I stood on the word, I walked myself out of that cancer." She now has a clean bill of health!

How did she do that? I didn't just lay hands on her and suddenly she had an instantaneous miracle. She walked herself out of that one day at a time speaking the Word. This is what I'm teaching you to do. Stop waiting for someone to come to town to lay hands on you for your healing. That's for new and immature Christians. Stand on the Word yourself.

Babies have to be spoon-fed—grownups feed themselves.

People use the 1 Corinthians chapter 2 passage to convince us that we don't really need preaching and teaching. They want us to believe that what we really need is a lot of praise and worship and many miracles. After all, Paul did not say that his speech and his preaching were not with persuasive words of human wisdom, but only demonstrations of the Spirit and power. That's not what this says. The subject of verse four is speech. It says, "My speech and preaching were not with persuasive words of human wisdom, but my *speech and preaching* were in demonstration of the spirit of power." Preaching needs to demonstrate the Spirit and power, not just lofty, persuasive words.

1 Corinthians 2:6 tells us, "*However, we speak wisdom among those who are mature, yet not the wisdom of this age, nor of the rulers of this age, who are coming to nothing. But we speak the wisdom of God in a mystery, the hidden wisdom which God ordained before the ages for our glory, which none of the rulers of this age knew; for had they known, they would not have crucified the Lord of glory. But as it is written: 'Eye has not seen, nor ear heard, nor have entered into the heart of man the things which God has prepared for those who love Him.'*"

Verse seven says, *"we speak the word of God in a mystery."* It goes on to say, *"none of the rulers of this age knew."* In other words, the demonic rulers of this world did not know what we were going to speak because if they had known what we were going to speak, they would never have crucified the Lord of glory.

It's the same thing that happens to you. The devil would never mess with you if he had known what was going to come out of your mouth. What are you going to say? "Oh, woe is me. I'm having such a hard time. I'm so sick. I think I'm going to die. Oh, I think we're going to go bankrupt." Is that what you're going to say? Because if you say that, Satan will make it harder and harder.

Instead, say, "By the stripes of Jesus, I was healed." If the devil knew you were going to stick to that confession, he would never have instigated the problems you're dealing with. The good news is that the Bible says God will take what the devil meant for evil and use it for good in your life. He will use it for good in the lives of others, even though He didn't cause it. He won't waste a single moment of your life, and you will become even more powerful.

Verse 12 promises, *"Now we have received not the spirit of the world, but the spirit who is from God."*

God gave the children of Israel the Promised Land, yet they had to go in and take it. God has given you healing, harvest, deliverance, and a sound mind, and yet you have to speak them. Scripture says, in verse 13, *"that we might know the things that have freely been given to us by God, these things also, we speak not in words, which man's wisdom teaches, but which the holy spirit teaches comparing spiritual things with spiritual."*

Look at the next verse. *"But the natural man does not receive the things of the spirit of God for they are foolishness to him."* This text talks about speaking the things that we have been given freely by God. Scripture says the natural man can't receive this. Some people think we're stark raving mad. Some people believe this is absolutely crazy. "You're going to what? You're just going to speak a few Bible verses, and God's going to what?"

Yes—that's what the Bible says!

Now, most of the time that's not all there is to it. Sometimes speaking the word opens a door of opportunity you need to walk through. Don't just sit at home with your feet propped up, watching TV, sipping lemonade saying, "Money, come to me!" and thinking it will show up in your lap.

The Bible says the natural man can't receive that. Some people on Christian television have not renewed their minds to the truth of the word of God concerning this. It's not that they're evil. It's not that they hate God. It's not that they're not trying, but they can't grasp it because they have not renewed their mind with the Word. You may say, "Well, this doesn't make any sense." I'm not here to talk to intellectuals about things that make sense. I'm here to talk to thinking people about comparing what it says in Scripture. We need to compare spiritual things to spiritual things. This makes no sense to the natural mind.

Some of you are healed because you talked to your body and you said, "Body, you will line up with the Word of God. No tumors or growths are going to develop in my body, but I'm going to be healed, healthy, and whole in the name of Jesus," and you stuck to that. That's why you have what you have. That's why you have your health today, and to the natural man, that makes no sense.

Absolutely no sense.

ELEVEN

"It Started with Your Words"

Here's the question we have to ask ourselves. What do we say when bad things happen? What do we say when we're dealing with the tough issues of life?

I'm not talking about mind over matter. I'm not talking about the power of positive thinking. I'm talking about the power of God at work in your life. That's what trips a lot of Christians up. I'm talking about the power of the Word of God and speaking the Word of God, just as God did in Genesis chapter one when he said, *"'Let there be light' and there was light."*

Again, in Mark 11:23, He says, *"Truly I tell you, if anyone says to this mountain, 'Go, throw yourself into the sea,' and does not doubt in their heart but believes that what they say will happen, it will be done for them."*

What do *we* say?

First of all, when you're having financial challenges, never say we don't have the money. We do that often with our children. Your children want this, your children want that and we say, "Well, we don't have the money." That's not a good thing to say. Do you know what your children need to hear? They need to hear "No" from you once in a while even if you have the money.

I saw a child pitching a fit in the grocery store the other day. He had a piece of candy clenched in his fist. His mother tried to take it away, saying, "I don't have the money. I don't have the money. I don't have the money." She should have looked that child in the face and said, "No. Even if I have a million dollars in the bank, you can't have that 50-cent piece of candy. No."

Often, we try to blame having to say no to our children on our lack of money. Our children grow up thinking if you have the money, then they will get what they want, and if you don't have the money, they don't get it. It's time for you to say, "I'm the parent. You're the child. It's none of your business how much money I have. You can't have that." So don't use, "I don't have the money," as an excuse. Grow up and be the parent.

It's okay to say, "We're not going to buy it right now." They don't have to know that you're hoping to get through the checkout counter and buy your groceries. You don't want your children growing up with a poverty mentality because, by the time they get old enough to know what's going on, you're going to be blessed, aren't you? So just tell them you're not going to buy that right now.

You need to be speaking Philippians 4:19, *"My God supplies all my need."* Speak the word. *"My God supplies all my need according to His riches and glory by Christ. Jesus."* You need to say that.

Let's talk about dealing with creditors. If creditors call, they are not interested in a faith-based answer. They want the facts. We're not lying. We're talking about the difference between the facts and the truth, and the facts and the truth are not always the same things. The fact may be the doctor saying you're dying of cancer, but the truth of the word of God says by His stripes, you were healed.

Jesus says, "My Word is truth." So, when we speak the Word of God in the face of adverse circumstances, we're not lying. We're speaking the truth, which often is not the same as the facts. For example, if you're three months behind on your house payment and your bank calls you about the amount, they don't want the truth. They want the facts. Don't tell them, "In the name of Jesus, I'll mail it tomorrow by faith."

It would be best if you told them the facts. I worked collections for a major bank for five years, so I understand what I'm talking about. These collectors are not your enemy. The only reason these guys seem like your enemies is that you treat them like dirt. If you treat them like decent human beings and recognize they could help you, most will try. I realize there are jerks out there. But most of them would help you if you would treat them with respect.

Once that collector hangs up from you and calls somebody else, he has forgotten he even talked to you. He's not constantly speaking negatively over your finances. He's just doing a job. When you say, "You know, I don't have the payment, I got laid off," or, "My unemployment check should be here soon, but I have a job interview tomorrow," you're telling him the facts. He's going to take those facts, and he's going to use them to try to help you, but he's going to forget he talked to you. Fifteen minutes later, he's not going to remember who you are because he's going to talk to 125 people in one day. You don't have to be concerned about him speaking negative words over you.

This is different from explaining the whole situation to a relative who meddles. If you have meddling parents or in-laws, they're the people you don't want to know because they're not going to forget you. You're probably the only project they have. "Sam, our daughter Betsy just called, and they're three months behind on their house payment. They're going down the tubes, Sam. Should we help? Sam, Betsy, just called again. It's not looking good. They're going to have to file for bankruptcy. I knew it. I told the children to be more careful with their money and to stop tithing to their church, but they wouldn't listen." They'll say that over you a hundred times, and you will have a negative declaration to deal with. That's different than dealing with your creditor. Give your creditor the facts and everybody else the truth.

Don't say that you can't lose weight. Stop speaking that over yourself because you never get anywhere that way. Your declaration needs to be based on the Word. Look at 1 Corinthians 9:27. It says, *"No, I strike a blow to my body and make it my slave so that after I have preached to others, I myself will not be disqualified for the prize."* We even have Christians trying to cast calories out of food!

The opposite of "I can't lose weight" is not "I'm sitting here in front of the TV, eating potato chips, drinking soda, not exercising, and I'm losing weight in the Name of Jesus." That's not the opposite of "I can't lose weight." The opposite is, *"I bring my body into subjection, and I discipline my body to make it do what it should do."*

Isn't it amazing the way Christians run from discipline? If you find a weight loss book and go to the introduction, and if it says you can lose weight with no exercise, with no need to make adjustments to your diet, throw that thing in the trash. It's a lie. Do you know what got you into this mess? It started with your *words.* You need to discipline yourself and acknowledge there are certain things you should never eat again and realize there are things you will need to do every day.

We're always looking for the easy way. Listen, the opposite of "I can't lose weight" is "I discipline my body, and I make my body do what it's supposed to do. I get the proper amount of exercise. I eat the right things. I stay away from junk food, get the right amount of sleep, and I'm refreshed every day. I get up with energy, and I serve God. I can do anything God's called me to do because of all the energy I have from disciplining my body." See, that's the confession you want, not, "I cast out these calories in the name of Jesus." That sounds good, but it's not the Bible. Then you can also declare, "I'm at my ideal weight."

Don't say, "I feel so sick. Oh, I'm so sick. I just feel so sick." Romans 8:11 says that the Spirit of God energizes your body. Say, "The spirit of God energizes me, and I feel great." 1 Peter 2:24 says that you are healed by the stripes of Jesus. Remember, talking to your doctor is very similar to talking to your creditors. The doctor needs to know the facts. You don't respond to the doctor's question of how you are feeling by saying, "By the stripes of Jesus, I'm healed." He'll ask, "So why are you here?" He can't help you with that.

When you go to the doctor, you're going to have to give them the facts. You give everybody else the truth. You give your neighbors the truth. "By the stripes of Jesus, I was healed," not, "I'm dying of cancer, and I have six months to live," because they'll say that a dozen times over you.

Some may say, "My husband is unresponsive," or "My husband is ungodly." Don't say that over your husband. Instead, say, "My husband loves me as he loves his own body. My husband covers me with prayer. My husband loves me and cares for me even as Christ also loves and cares for the church." That's what you need to be speaking over your husband.

Don't say about your children, "My children are rebellious and will not obey me." Don't say that. You need to start with your words. And just like Moses whacked that rock with the rod of God, some of your children need discipline. After you speak the word over them, you may need to discipline them, in love of course!

Ephesians 6:1-3 has a great confession which says, *"Children obey your parents in the Lord for this is right. They honor their father and mother, which is the first commandment with promise so that it may be well with them and they may live long on the earth."* That's what you need to be saying to and over your children.

You shouldn't say, "I can't succeed in my business. My business is not succeeding. My business is not doing well. I think my business is going to go down the tubes." Don't say that over your business and then hope for a miracle. So often we say negative things, and we hope God will deliver us from what we say! Instead, based on Proverbs 22:29, we should say: *"I excel in my business!"*

Hopefully by now you are beginning to see the importance of the atmosphere you create around you with your words. Let me finish by encouraging you to speak God's Word over your life at every opportunity. When you're getting ready for your day, have index cards with scriptures from the following chapter for you to speak out loud to start your morning. Put more cards on the dashboard of your car and speak them on the way to work. I even know a couple that used a permanent marker to write verses on the glass door of their shower! Make a quality decision *right now* to change the way you talk. In six months, you might not even recognize the "old you" anymore as you're overtaken by the blessings of God!

TWELVE

"Topical Faith Declarations"

If words got us into the situations in which we find ourselves, and words can get us out—what should we actually say? The following declarations are taken directly from Scripture, so that you can be speaking exactly what the Word of God says about you and your circumstances.

These Bible verses and declarations aren't "magic," and often you won't see instantaneous results. However, you will soon begin to see a change in your thinking, then in your heart, and finally in your outward circumstances, as you create an atmosphere of faith around you with your words.

Of course, this is not even close to an exhaustive list of Scriptures or topics. I've written these faith declarations to get you started, but you're going to want to use the concordance at the back of your Bible or a Topical Bible to do your own research and make your own list of Powerful Scriptures to fit your particular situation.

I highly recommend that you don't wait until attacks come to start making these declarations over your life. Rather, set aside just a few minutes each day to make a couple of the declarations in each category to keep your heart, mind, and focus strong. When you do that, you will be amazed at how much more prepared you are when life takes an unexpected turn.

Stand strong with His Word in your mouth!

The Power of Your Words

What the Bible says: *"A man's stomach shall be satisfied from the fruit of his mouth; From the produce of his lips he shall be filled."* —Proverbs 18:20

What *you* say: *"I speak words that are satisfying to my soul. My words produce a life that is filled with the goodness and provision of God!"*

What the Bible says: *"Death and life are in the power of the tongue, And those who love it will eat its fruit."* —Proverbs 18:21

What *you* say: *"Either death and destruction, or life and blessing will manifest in my life because of the words that I choose. I choose words of life, health, and blessing!"*

What the Bible says: *"There is one who speaks like the piercings of a sword, But the tongue of the wise promotes health."*—Proverbs 12:18

What *you* say: *"I choose my words wisely, and those words are based upon God's Words. I choose to operate in the Wisdom of God as I speak His Word, and His Word produces life and health!"*

What the Bible says: *"The heart of the wise teaches his mouth, And adds learning to his lips. Pleasant words are like a honeycomb, Sweetness to the soul and health to the bones."* —Prov. 16:23-24

What *you* say: *"I don't just speak the first words that come to my mind, rather I teach my mouth to speak Words of Life from God's Word. My words are pleasant and sweet like honey to my soul, and those words cause health and strength to my bones!"*

What the Bible says: *"For assuredly, I say to you, whoever says to this mountain, 'Be removed and be cast into the sea,' and does not doubt in his heart, but believes that those things he says will be done, he will have whatever he says."*—Mark 11:23

What *you* say: *"My words, based upon God's Word, have power! I don't doubt in my heart, but I believe that those things that I SAY will come to pass!"*

What the Bible says: *"For out of the abundance of the heart the mouth speaks. A good man out of the good treasure of his heart brings forth good things."*—Matthew 12:34-35

What *you* say: *"I store up the treasure of God's Word in my heart, so that when I sense the pressures of life closing in, my mouth speaks from the abundance of that treasure! Speaking The Word of God into my circumstances produces good things in my life!"*

What the Bible says: *"Let us hold fast the confession of our hope without wavering, for He who promised is faithful."* —Hebrews 10:23

What *you* say: *"I hold fast to my declaration of God's Word, and refuse to allow the circumstances of life to rob me of the promises of God!"*

What the Bible says: *"And since we have the same spirit of faith, according to what is written, 'I believed and therefore I spoke,' we also believe and therefore speak,"*—II Corinthians 4:13

What *you* say: *"I declare that I am filled with the Spirit of Faith in God and His Word! I refuse to focus on any circumstances that attack me. I believe and speak the unchanging Word of God!"*

What the Bible says: *"A man shall eat well by the fruit of his mouth, But the soul of the unfaithful feeds on violence. He who guards his mouth preserves his life, But he who opens wide his lips shall have destruction."*—Proverbs 13:2-3

What *you* say: *"I refuse to allow my mouth to speak destruction to my life! I guard my mouth and discipline it to speak God's Word in every circumstance. I eat well because of the fruit of the words that I speak!"*

What the Bible says: *"So shall My word be that goes forth from My mouth; It shall not return to Me void, But it shall accomplish what I please, And it shall prosper in the thing for which I sent it."* —Isaiah 55:11

What *you* say: *"God's Word will not return to Him empty, but will absolutely produce His Perfect Will every time. I speak His Word in agreement with Him, and those Words produce God's Perfect Will in my life every time I speak them!"*

Healing and Health

What the Bible says: *"Beloved, I pray that you may prosper in all things and be in health, just as your soul prospers."*—III John 2

What *you* say: *"I declare today that just as my soul continues to grow in God and in His Word, my daily life prospers in every way, and health and healing are mine!"*

What the Bible says: *"Then Jesus went about all the cities and villages, teaching in their synagogues, preaching the Gospel of the Kingdom, and healing EVERY sickness and EVERY disease among the people."* —Matt. 9:35

What the Bible says: *"Jesus Christ is the same yesterday, today, and forever."*—Hebrews 13:8

What *you* say: *"Every sickness and every disease that attacks my body comes to naught. Jesus Christ is the same yesterday, today, and forever, and He is still healing today by the Power of His Word!"*

What the Bible says: *"Who Himself bore our sins in His Own Body on the tree, that we, having died to sins, might live for righteousness—by Whose Stripes you were healed."*—1 Peter 2:24, and *"Who forgives all your iniquities, Who heals all your diseases."* —Psalm 103:3

What *you* say: *"My healing is a part of the atonement that Jesus paid for on the cross, that I might continue to live for righteousness. By His Stripes I was healed!"*

What the Bible says: *"And He said, If you diligently heed the Voice of the Lord Your God and do what is right in His Sight, give ear to His Commands, and keep all His Statutes, I will put none of the diseases on you which I have brought on the Egyptians. For I am the Lord Who heals you."*—Exodus 15:26

What *you* say: *"I listen diligently to the Voice of the Lord, do what is right in His sight, and give serious attention to His Word. God doesn't put any disease on me, for He is the Lord Who heals me!"*

What the Bible says: *"But if the Spirit of Him Who raised Jesus from the dead dwells in you, He Who raised Christ from the dead will also give life to your mortal bodies through His Spirit Who dwells in you."*—Romans 8:11

What *you* say: *"I declare that the same Spirit Who raised Christ from the dead lives in me, and makes my mortal body alive, strong, and vibrant!"*

What the Bible says: *"So you shall serve the Lord your God, and He will bless your bread and your water. And I will take sickness away from the midst of you."*—Exodus 23:25

What *you* say: *"I declare today that I am your committed servant. Thank you for Your promise to bless my food and drink, and to remove sickness from my midst!"*

What the Bible says: *"Bless the Lord, O my soul, And forget not all His benefits: Who forgives all your iniquities, Who heals all your diseases, Who redeems your life from destruction, Who crowns you with lovingkindness and tender mercies, Who satisfies your mouth with good things, So that your youth is renewed like the eagle's."*—Psalm 103:2-5

What *you* say: *"I declare today that just as all of my sins are forgiven by Jesus' finished work on the cross, all of my diseases are paid for as well! My life is redeemed from destruction, and my youth is renewed as the eagle's!"*

What the Bible says: *"Then they cried out to the Lord in their trouble, And He saved them out of their distresses. He sent His word and healed them, And delivered them from their destructions."*—Ps. 107:19-20

What *you* say: *"I keep God's Word on my lips continually. He sent His Word to heal me and to deliver me from any destruction that the enemy has planned for me. Healing is mine!"*

What the Bible says: *"He gives power to the weak, And to those who have no might He increases strength. Even the youths shall faint and be weary, And the young men shall utterly fall, But those who wait on the Lord Shall renew their strength; They shall mount up with wings like eagles, They shall run and not be weary, They shall walk and not faint."*— Isaiah 40:29-31

What *you* say: *"God gives me His power and renews my strength. I will not faint or be overcome with weariness. God's vitality operates within me!"*

What the Bible says: *"My son, give attention to my words; Incline your ear to my sayings. Do not let them depart from your eyes; Keep them in the midst of your heart; For they are life to those who find them, And health to all their flesh."*—Proverbs 4:20-22

What *you* say: *"I give attention to the Word Of God and keep the Word before me, in my heart, and in my mouth at all times. God's Word is life and health!"*

Money and Finances

What the Bible says: *"The Lord is my Shepherd; I shall not want."*—Psalms 23:1

What *you* say: *"The Lord is my Shepherd. As I follow His leading and direction, He provides for everything I need."*

What the Bible says: *"Oh, taste and see that the Lord is good; Blessed is the man who trusts in Him! Oh, fear the Lord, you His saints! There is no want to those who fear Him. The young lions lack and suffer hunger; But those who seek the Lord shall not lack any good thing."*—Psalm 34:8-10

What *you* say: *"God has been so good to me! I am blessed because I put my trust in Him, and I don't lack any good thing!"*

What the Bible says: *"Beloved, I pray that you may prosper in all things and be in health, just as your soul prospers."*—III John 1:2

What *you* say: *"As my soul continues to grow in the Grace of God, I prosper in everything that I do!"*

What the Bible says: *"Give, and it will be given to you: good measure, pressed down, shaken together, and running over will be put into your bosom. For with the same measure that you use, it will be measured back to you."*—Luke 6:38

What *you* say: *"I am a generous giver…and I can't out-give God! As I am a blessing to others and to my Church. God continues to bless me abundantly!"*

What the Bible says: *"And my God shall supply all your need according to His riches in glory by Christ Jesus."*—Philippians 4:19

What *you* say: *"God supplies everything I need according to His unlimited supply and ability!"*

What the Bible says: *"Therefore do not worry, saying, 'What shall we eat?' or 'What shall we drink?' or 'What shall we wear?' For after all these things the Gentiles seek. For your heavenly Father knows that you need all these things. But seek first the kingdom of God and His righteousness, and all these things shall be added to you."*—Matthew 6:31-33

What *you* say: *"I don't spend my time worrying about my daily needs, because my Heavenly Father knows the things that I need. Instead, I seek first the Kingdom of God and develop my relationship with Him, and he adds everything to my life that I need!"*

What the Bible says: *"This Book of the Law shall not depart from your mouth, but you shall meditate in it day and night, that you may observe to do according to all that is written in it. For then you will make your way prosperous, and then you will have good success."*—Joshua 1:8

What *you* say: *"I am focused on the Word of God. I declare the Word, meditate in the Word, and obey the Word! By doing these things, I ensure that my way is prosperous and I am successful!"*

What the Bible says: *"Honor the Lord with your possessions, And with the first fruits of all your increase; So your barns will be filled with plenty, And your vats will overflow with new wine."*—Proverbs 3:9-10

What *you* say: *"I honor the Lord with my possessions and with the first of my income. My life is full to overflowing with the goodness of God!"*

What the Bible says: *"But this I say: He who sows sparingly will also reap sparingly, and he who sows bountifully will also reap bountifully. And God is able to make all grace abound toward you, that you, always having all sufficiency in all things, may have an abundance for every good work."*—II Corinthians 9:6-8

What *you* say: *"I am a bountiful sower, so I reap the bountiful grace of God! I have abundance for every need and good work, and every need I have is met in Him!"*

What the Bible says: *"Bring all the tithes into the storehouse, That there may be food in My house, And try Me now in this,' Says the Lord of hosts, 'If I will not open for you the windows of heaven And pour out for you such blessing That there will not be room enough to receive it. And I will rebuke the devourer for your sakes, So that he will not destroy the fruit of your ground, Nor shall the vine fail to bear fruit for you in the field,' Says the Lord of hosts; 'And all nations will call you blessed, For you will be a delightful land,' Says the Lord of hosts."*—Malachi 3:10-12

What *you* say: *"As I bring the full tithe, 10% of my income, to my Church, there is always spiritual food in the House Of God. The blessings of heaven are poured out on me in abundance, and the enemy is rebuked for my sake, and he cannot bring destruction to any part of my life. The blessing of God on me is evidence to everyone around me of God's goodness!"*

Marriage and Family

What the Bible says: *"Therefore a man shall leave his father and mother and be joined to his wife, and they shall become one flesh."*—Genesis 2:24

What *you* say: *"Even though my spouse and I honor our parents, we have left their homes, care, and covering. We are now joined together, completely committed to one another as husband and wife. We are inseparable!"*

What the Bible says: *"Husbands, love your wives, just as Christ also loved the church and gave Himself for her... So husbands ought to love their own wives as their own bodies; he who loves his wife loves himself."*—Ephesians 5:25 & 28

What *you* say (husbands): *"I love my wife and give up my life for her, just as Christ gave Himself up for His Bride, the Church. I love my wife as much as I value my own life!"*

What *you* say (wives): *"My husband loves me and gives up his life for me, just as Christ gave Himself up for His Bride, the Church. My husband loves me as much as he values his own life!"*

What the Bible says: *"Nevertheless let each one of you in particular so love his own wife as himself, and let the wife see that she respects her husband."*—Ephesians 5:33

What *you* say: *"My (husband/wife) and I love each other dearly, and we respect each other's opinions, thoughts, and our individual walks with God."*

What the Bible says: *"Husbands, likewise, dwell with them with understanding, giving honor to the wife, as to the weaker vessel, and as being heirs together of the grace of life, that your prayers may not be hindered."*—I Peter 3:7

What *you* say (husbands): *"I live with my wife as we seek understanding together in the affairs of this life. I give honor to her because we are heirs together of God's Grace, and the answers to my prayers are not hindered in any way."*

What *you* say (wives): *"My husband and I seek understanding together in the affairs of this life. My husband honors me because we are heirs together of God's Grace, and his prayers are never hindered in any way."*

What the Bible says: *"Wives, likewise, be submissive to your own husbands, that even if some do not obey the word, they, without a word, may be won by the conduct of their wives, when they observe your chaste conduct accompanied by fear. Do not let your adornment be merely outward—arranging the hair, wearing gold, or putting on fine apparel— rather let it be the hidden person of the heart, with the incorruptible beauty of a gentle and quiet spirit, which is very precious in the sight of God."* —I Peter 3:1-4

What *you* say (wives): *"I respect my husband, realizing that the way I live my life and relate to him is a powerful influence in his life. I not only pay attention to my outward appearance, but also give attention to my heart. I cultivate the incorruptible beauty of a gentle and quiet spirit, which is very precious in the sight of God and my husband."*

What the Bible says: *"Let the husband render to his wife the affection due her, and likewise also the wife to her husband. The wife does not have authority over her own body, but the husband does. And likewise the husband does not have authority over his own body, but the wife does. Do not deprive one another except with consent for a time, that you may give yourselves to fasting and prayer; and come together again so that Satan does not tempt you because of your lack of self-control."*—I Corinthians 7:3-5

What *you* say: *"We give each other the intimate affection that each desires, realizing that our spouse has a marital right to that attention. We are never demanding, always loving and willing, and never withhold intimacy as a weapon."*

What the Bible says: *"Marriage is honorable among all, and the bed undefiled; but fornicators and adulterers God will judge."*—Hebrews 13:4

What *you* say: *"Our marriage bed and intimate moments are exclusively OURS. We enjoy our intimate times together, and never allow ourselves to look outside of our marriage relationship for affection or attention."*

What the Bible says: *"Train up a child in the way he should go, And when he is old he will not depart from it."*—Proverbs 22:6

What *you* say: *"We train up our children in the ways of God by taking them to Church, participating in worship and prayer together, and by taking advantage of 'life lesson' moments at home. When our children become adults and 'grow up', they will continue in the ways of God that we have taught them!"*

What the Bible says: *"'Children, obey your parents in the Lord, for this is right. Honor your father and mother,' which is the first commandment with promise: 'that it may be well with you and you may live long on the earth.'"* Ephesians 6:1-3

What *you* say: *"Our children obey their parents. They honor their father and mother, and inherit the promise of long life on the earth!"*

What the Bible says: *"Let all bitterness, wrath, anger, clamor, and evil speaking be put away from you, with all malice. And be kind to one another, tenderhearted, forgiving one another, even as God in Christ forgave you."*—Ephesians 4:31-32

What *you* say: *"My spouse and I refuse to allow bitterness, anger, hurtful words, and malice to take root in our relationship. When we catch ourselves in any disrespectful behavior, we commit ourselves to immediately arrest it! We are instead kind to one another, tender hearted, ready to forgive and ask for forgiveness, just as Christ has readily forgiven us!"*

Peace and Strength

What the Bible says: *"You will keep him in perfect peace, Whose mind is stayed on You, Because he trusts in You."*—Isaiah 26:3

What *you* say: *"I keep my mind focused on the Lord. As I trust Him with all of the affairs of my life, I spend my days in perfect peace no matter what is happening around me."*

What the Bible says: *"Be anxious for nothing, but in everything by prayer and supplication, with thanksgiving, let your requests be made known to God; and the peace of God, which surpasses all understanding, will guard your hearts and minds through Christ Jesus."*—Philippians 4:6-7

What *you* say: *"I refuse to allow anxiety to get a hold of my mind and heart, but instead give thanks to God for my life, and make my requests known to Him in prayer. God's peace, which is so great that I can't even comprehend it, guards my heart and mind through Christ Jesus!"*

What the Bible says: *"Peace I leave with you, My peace I give to you; not as the world gives do I give to you. Let not your heart be troubled, neither let it be afraid."*—John 14:27

What *you* say: *"I refuse to allow my heart to be troubled or fearful. I have God's peace on the inside, which is greater than any circumstance or challenge that I experience in the world around me!"*

What the Bible says: *"And let the peace of God rule in your hearts, to which also you were called in one body; and be thankful."*—Colossians 3:15

What *you* say: *"I am so thankful for the Peace Of God that rules and reigns in my heart! I am called to spread that Peace to all those I come in contact with in the Body of Christ!"*

What the Bible says: *"that He would grant you, according to the riches of His glory, to be strengthened with might through His Spirit in the inner man, that Christ may dwell in your hearts through faith; that you, being rooted and grounded in love,"*—Ephesians 3:16-17

What *you* say: *"I am strengthened with might through the Spirit of God Who lives inside of me according to the riches Of God! Christ dwells in my heart through faith, and I am rooted and grounded in His Love!"*

What the Bible says: *"I can do all things through Christ who strengthens me."*—Philippians 4:13

What *you* say: *"I can do everything that God has called me to do, and I can take advantage of every opportunity that the Spirit of God presents to me, through the strength and power of Christ in me!"*

What the Bible says: *"Fear not, for I am with you; Be not dismayed, for I am your God. I will strengthen you, Yes, I will help you, I will uphold you with My righteous right hand."* —Isaiah 41:10

What *you* say: *"I refuse to walk in fear because God is with me and He is MY God! He will strengthen me, He will help me, and He will uphold me with His righteous right hand!"*

What the Bible says: *"He gives power to the weak, And to those who have no might He increases strength. Even the youths shall faint and be weary, And the young men shall utterly fall, But those who wait on the Lord Shall renew their strength; They shall mount up with wings like eagles, They shall run and not be weary, They shall walk and not faint."* —Isaiah 40:29-31

What *you* say: *"Even on days when I feel weak, I refuse to allow that weakness to take hold in my mind and heart, because God is increasing my strength every day! I wait daily on the Lord in prayer, and He renews my strength! My days are not filled with weariness or fainting, but instead I mount up over the circumstances of this life with wings like eagles!"*

What the Bible says: *"The Lord is my light and my salvation; Whom shall I fear? The Lord is the strength of my life; Of whom shall I be afraid?"*—Psalm 27:1

What *you* say: *"The Lord is my light, my salvation, and the strength of my life. I am not afraid of anyone or anything!"*

Made in the USA
Middletown, DE
09 February 2023

24221885R00076